Thinking Room

Where Noticing Begins

Joanna Joustra

Praise for Joanna Joustra

You can feel the author's kindness, wisdom, and helpfulness on every page. Step by step, warmly and easily, Joanna guides us to find inner quiet, strength and happiness – that we so need these noisy days.

— Rick Hanson, PhD, Author of
Hardwiring Happiness

Joanna provides simple tools that enhance clarity of thought, bringing more awareness of the choices we have over the stories we tell ourselves, the life we want to live and the person we aspire to be. Could not recommend more.

— Amazon Book Review

So much of the book has enlightened me, and switched on parts of my consciousness that I never knew existed.

— Google Review

Copyright © 2026 by Joanna Joustra

All rights reserved.

No part of this book may be reproduced in any form or by any electronic or mechanical means, including information storage and retrieval systems, without written permission from the author, except for the use of brief quotations in a book review.

yarravalleycounselling.com.au

Contents

1. The Room — 1
2. Inside — 8
3. Reaction — 15
4. The System — 24
5. Capacity — 30
6. Pressure — 39
7. Story — 48
8. Staying — 57
9. Threshold — 65
10. Here — 71

Chapter One

The Room

There are times when life looks settled on the outside, yet your mind refuses to stand down.

It might be late at night, after an ordinary day. Your body is tired enough to sleep, yet something in you is still alert. The lights are off, the house is quiet, and the day is technically over. Your mind disagrees. It replays a conversation you thought you'd already filed away. It rewinds a moment and holds it up from a new angle. It searches for what you missed. It rehearses the next interaction as if you're about to walk into it any minute, even if it might never happen.

It might be driving somewhere familiar, arriving at your destination and realising you barely remember the trip. Your hands did what they've always done. Your eyes watched the road. Your mind was elsewhere, busy in a private loop of planning, reviewing, predicting, and fixing. You step out of the car and feel a strange lag in your body, as though you've been travelling for longer than you have.

Thinking Room

It might be sitting with people you care about, laughing at the right moments, nodding in the right places, hearing the words they're saying and yet also tracking something else underneath. What you said. What you should have said. The pause that felt too long. The look that seemed slightly off. Whether you were too much. Whether you were not enough. Whether you have done something wrong.

Nothing dramatic is happening. There is no obvious crisis. The day might even look good on paper.

Inside, something feels busy. Tight. Heavy. A little too full.

When this becomes familiar, it makes sense to reach for solutions. Thoughtful, capable people do what thoughtful, capable people do. They try to solve it. They read. They listen. They reflect. They become productive. They stay one step ahead of the discomfort. They try to calm down in all the ways the world recommends. Meditation apps. Exercise routines. Gratitude lists. Journals. Podcasts that promise a new way of thinking. Fresh starts that feel hopeful for a few days.

Some of it works, briefly.

Then the familiar current returns. The same corridors. The same loops. The same sense of being inside your head, even when you would rather be inside your life.

Over time, a quieter question begins to form. It doesn't arrive with drama or urgency. It arrives with fatigue.

Why does my mind keep doing this?

A second question follows, a little more tender, a little more exposed.

The Room

Is there another way to be with my inner world that doesn't leave me either tangled in it or running from it?

Many people assume the struggle is the content of their thoughts. If I could just stop overthinking. If I could just let things go. If I could just settle. The mind becomes the enemy and the day becomes a constant negotiation. You argue with yourself. You reason. You motivate. You promise you will do better. You try to be more disciplined. You try to be more resilient.

A different possibility begins to surface when the usual strategies stop working. The deeper pattern might sit underneath the thoughts themselves, in the way your system is organised, in what your brain is trying to do, in what your body is carrying. A mind that won't settle is rarely a mind that is simply being difficult. It is often a mind doing its best to manage something, prepare for something, protect you from something, or keep you functioning under a load that has quietly grown.

A new way to understand this begins with an image.

Imagine your mind, or your inner world, as a room.

A lived-in room. The kind that tells the truth. Papers spread across the table. Notes you meant to deal with later. Old memories stacked in corners like boxes you never quite unpacked. Half-finished conversations left open, like tabs you forgot to close. Future plans scribbled in the margins. There might be a chair you always end up in, the one you collapse into when you cannot do any more. There might be parts of the room you avoid, areas that feel crowded or tender or too full of history.

Thinking Room

Some days this room feels workable. You can move. You can think. You can respond. You can breathe.

Other days it feels crowded, loud, or hard to breathe in. It can feel as though the room has shrunk around you. Thoughts press close. Every small task feels heavier than it should. You find yourself searching for the right thought that will make it all make sense and lift the weight, as though the right explanation might restore the air.

Most of us try to improve life inside this room by rearranging what's in it. We argue with ourselves. We explain. We justify. We criticise. We motivate. We rehearse. We chase certainty. We try to get the room to feel better by moving the furniture around while we are still standing in the middle of it.

It is exhausting work.

It is also familiar work, especially if you learned early that thinking hard was the safest way to cope. Some people became good at problem-solving. Some became good at anticipating. Some became good at managing other people's expectations. Some became good at holding it together. These strengths often look impressive from the outside. Inside, they can feel like a room that never really rests.

What changes things, quietly, is discovering there is more than one place to stand.

You may have touched this before without naming it. A brief pause where you realise, I'm thinking again. A moment where you notice the loop instead of being pulled by it. A flicker of space when something softens, even slightly, like a window cracked open after a long night of stale air.

These moments come and go. They can feel almost accidental.

They matter.

They are the first sign that the room can be entered differently. The first sign that you are not only the one living inside the room, but also the one who can notice it. That noticing is not an achievement. It is something already present in you, even if you have only felt it in glimpses.

Understanding overthinking begins there.

It begins with the possibility that your mind is not a problem to solve, but a place you can learn to understand. A place with its own architecture, habits, and protective reflexes. Once you can see how the room is built, what tends to light up, what tends to echo, what gets stored in the corners, you stop taking every passing thought as an instruction. You become less surprised by your own patterns. You start to recognise what is happening in real time, before it takes over the whole space.

Overthinking, worry, mental busyness, and emotional swings are not random faults in your character. They are patterns that arise from a system doing its best to keep you safe, efficient, and prepared. Seeing this does something gentle but significant. The room stops feeling like a personal indictment. Your experience begins to make sense.

Relief rarely arrives because you finally win an argument with your mind. Relief arrives when you begin to relate to the room with a little more space and a little less urgency. You learn what helps the air move through again. You learn what escalates the noise. You learn what steadies you, and

Thinking Room

what drains you. You learn how to return to yourself without needing to become someone else.

This is the thinking room. A room you can learn to understand. A room you can learn to live in with more ease.

A room that becomes less frightening when you stop believing you have to control every sound inside it.

Once you know where you are standing in relation to the room, the rest of the journey begins to make sense.

And you are not doing this alone.

Your body's sensations are already in the room with you, shaping the light, shaping the air, shaping what feels possible, long before you've had time to think a thought all the way through.

Reflection

As you read this, where do you recognise yourself most clearly?

_____

_____

What have you already tried to quiet your mind, and what has that been like for you?

_____

_____

What time of day does your mind tend to ramp up most — and what do you usually do when it does?

_____

_____

Take your time with this. What you're beginning to notice isn't only happening in thought.

Before the mind explains, before the story forms, something else has already shifted.

The body often moves first, quietly, automatically and the mind follows, calling that movement "truth."

If you want to understand what happens next, this is where attention needs to turn.

Chapter Two

Inside

You are always in at least two rooms at once.

There is the room around you, the one with walls and light and objects you recognise. A kitchen bench with dishes gathering. A car interior warmed by sun. A bed with sheets you meant to change. A phone screen glowing on the table. A mug cooling beside you.

And there is the room inside your mind.

The inner room does not have walls you can touch, but you know it by feel. It is where you live from. Where thoughts gather themselves. Where memory wanders in, unannounced. Where you keep returning, sometimes without meaning to. It's the room you can't step out of, because it's the room you are living from.

Most of the time, the inner and outer rooms sit on top of each other so neatly you don't think to separate them. You move through the outer room while the inner room hums in the background, like a radio you've stopped noticing.

Inside

Until something changes.

It might be small enough to miss at first.

Your phone pings and you feel a quick lift in the chest before you've even looked. Someone's tone deepens by half a shade and your shoulders tighten, just slightly. A door closes somewhere in the house and the sound lands heavier than it should. You're driving a familiar road and suddenly realise your jaw has been clenched for kilometres. You're standing at the sink and the day, for no clear reason, feels like it has less air in it.

Nothing dramatic has happened in the outer room.

The kettle still boils. The traffic still moves. The light still falls where it always falls.

Yet inside, the inner room is no longer quite the same.

And this is where the body comes in. Quietly. Practically. Without any interest in explanation. It arrives as sensation, a physical signal that touches the inner room before the mind has decided what anything means.

A tightening behind the ribs.

A breath that lengthens to a sigh.

Heat rising into the face.

A heartbeat making itself known.

A heaviness that settles without permission.

These sensations are messages. Not the whole story, but the first stirring of it.

Thinking Room

They move through the inner room the way weather moves through a house, shifting the air, changing the light, altering what feels possible.

A tightening in the chest can feel like a sudden drop in temperature.

A shallow breath like the air thinning.

Heat climbing like pressure building before a storm.

A dull heaviness like light fading earlier than expected.

The outer room hasn't changed. The furniture of your life is still in place but the experience of being in it has.

The shift is subtle, and that's what makes it so confusing. You can be doing the same ordinary thing you always do, and suddenly the inner room feels closer, more crowded, slightly watchful. Thoughts that were passing through begin to stick. Sounds land more sharply. Time feels tighter. A simple task feels heavier in the hands.

And because the inner room is the place where meaning forms, weather shapes meaning too.

A passing comment that would have been neutral in clear air can land differently under heavy cloud. A pause can feel spacious one day and loaded the next. A glance can feel like nothing… or like something you should worry about. The same moment arrives, yet under different inner conditions it carries a different weight.

This is why the body speaks first.

Long before you can name what's happening, the system has already registered something: effort, uncertainty, demand, safety shifting. It responds in the only language it has.

Most of us were never taught to read this.

We were taught to look at the furniture instead. The thought. The meaning. The conclusion. We try to tidy the room by rearranging what's in it, while the weather continues to move through the space unseen.

When the inner atmosphere becomes uncomfortable, many of us pull the blinds. We brace. We push on. We close ourselves off from sensation because it feels inconvenient, or because it feels like too much.

Yet weather doesn't stop because we refuse to look at it. It keeps moving, and the room keeps being shaped.

There is no moment where the inner room exists on its own. No pure thinking space untouched by sensation. The room is always lived from the inside of a body that is responding in real time, shifting the light, changing the air, setting the conditions under which thought will form.

Sometimes the weather turns so quietly you don't notice until you're already living inside it.

A little less air. A little less room. A thought landing harder than it should. A tone that stings. A body already braced.

Other times it comes in fast, the drop, the rush, the tightening, and you name it immediately. Stress.

It doesn't always arrive with a reason you can point to. It can arrive as atmosphere. As pressure. As a change in how the room feels to be in.

When that's hard to see, the mind does what it always does. It looks for someone to blame.

Often it chooses you.

Why am I like this?

Why am I so reactive?

Why can't I get a grip?

And then, sometimes, you notice what's been true all along. The weather moved through first.

The body sent a signal before the mind assembled a story. A tightening. A shallowing. Heat rising. Energy dropping away. The inner room already shifting its light and air before you'd had time to make sense of why.

Nothing dramatic needs to happen in the outer room for this to be real. The day can stay ordinary. The kettle can boil. The phone can sit face down. Someone can speak in a neutral tone. Life can look unchanged, even as the inner atmosphere changes everything about how you receive it.

This is what noticing begins to reveal: a way to recognise the sequence.

Not so you can control the weather. Not so you can keep the room perfectly clear. Simply so you're no longer confused by the fact that your experience can change before you've "worked out" what's going on.

When you begin to see that inner weather often moves first, you stop treating the shift as a personal mystery. You begin to see it as a living pattern, one you've been inside for a long time, often without language for it. You're not making it up.

Inside

You're not "too much". You're not failing some invisible test of calm.

You're in a room that is always lived through weather.

Thinking Room

Reflection

When you notice yourself shifting, what's the first physical sign you tend to pick up (breath, chest, jaw, stomach, shoulders, energy)?

What are the most common everyday triggers for you (a text, a tone, being rushed, transitions, silence, end of day, social situations)?

What is your mind's first "headline thought" when that shift happens? (e.g., I've done something wrong / I'm behind / they're annoyed / this won't work out)

Once you start noticing these early signals, a pattern begins to emerge.

The shifts are not random. They arrive in clusters. They gather momentum. They change the atmosphere inside you long before anything looks different on the outside.

What you are learning to read now is not a single sensation, but a kind of inner weather — one that shapes how the day is carried from the inside out.

Chapter Three

Reaction

There is a particular kind of moment that many people only recognise once it has already passed.

A sentence leaves your mouth with an edge you didn't mean. Your body pulls back slightly, as if to create distance, before you've even worked out what you're distancing from. Irritation rises with a sudden heat that seems to arrive out of nowhere. Something sharp moves through you first, and only later does the thinking mind catch up and begin its familiar work of replaying, reviewing, and trying to understand what just happened.

Sometimes the outer room barely changes. A kitchen light, a lounge chair, a familiar face across the table. And yet the inner room has already tightened.

When things settle, the room looks different again. The air feels calmer. You can see more clearly. You imagine how you wish you had handled it, how you could have paused, chosen your words, stayed softer, responded with more patience. From this quieter vantage point, it can feel obvious. It can feel as though you should have known better. It can feel as though the version of you who reacted was careless, immature, or simply not trying hard enough.

Inside the moment, it rarely feels like that.

Inside your inner room, under shifting weather, the system moves at a speed that has nothing to do with your intelligence or your values. The reaction arrives before you have the sense of having any real say in it. It happens quickly because something in you has registered a change in conditions, and the body responds as it was designed to respond: by preparing. Not after careful thought. Before it. Not because you are dramatic. Because you are human.

Often nothing in the outer room changes in a way you could point to. The conversation continues. The kettle boils. The car moves along the same familiar stretch of road. Yet something shifts in the inner room all the same, and the weather moves through quickly enough that it can be hard to track. A tone deepens. A silence stretches. A look lands with a strange weight. It is subtle, the kind of detail you might not even mention if someone asked what happened, and yet it is enough to bring the body online. Breath shortens. The chest tightens. Muscles prepare. Attention narrows, just slightly at first, as if the room has begun looking for exits.

This is the part most people miss. Your nervous system does not wait for certainty. It works on likelihood.

When the air changes in the room, the mind begins gathering evidence at speed. It does not do this neatly, or deliberately, or in orderly sentences. It does it the way a living mind has always done it: by reaching into what it already knows. It pulls down old books from familiar shelves, the ones that have been handled many times before. A past conversation. A past hurt. The way someone once looked at you right before they withdrew. A memory of being misunderstood. The feeling of getting it wrong. These fragments are not always explicit. Sometimes they arrive as a faint sense of dread, or a tightening behind the eyes, or a wave of urgency that makes you want to fix something quickly.

The room begins to make meaning before you have agreed to any meaning.

The mind turns over the evidence quickly, not to torment you, but to protect you. It scans the moment and tries to decide what it resembles. It searches for patterns, not because you are overdramatic, but because your brain is built to predict what might happen next. It is built to anticipate. It is built to keep you ready. In that split second, it would rather prepare for something that might not happen than be caught unprepared if it does.

The mind doesn't wait. It leans forward. It guesses.

It works from likelihood, from what has happened before, and what it fears might happen again.

It can feel like you suddenly know what the pause means, what the tone means, what the silence means. It can feel like you suddenly understand the whole situation in a single instant, even if you cannot articulate how you got there. Your body moves as though the conclusion is already true. You brace. You withdraw. You sharpen. You explain yourself too quickly. You try to regain control. Or you shut down and go quiet, as if the room has grown too tight to speak in.

Thinking Room

When people look back and say, "I don't know why I reacted like that," it is often because the reaction began before the story could be traced. The system detected something and began preparing in advance, and by the time you were aware enough to reflect, the weather had already intensified.

From the outside, this can look like overreaction. From the inside, it is speed.

Choice takes time. It requires space. It requires a little steadiness in the air so that you can hold more than one possibility at once. Prediction does not operate that way. Prediction values immediacy. It values what has worked before. When the room feels charged or uncertain, the system does not pause to weigh options like a calm committee meeting. It moves first and explains later.

This is where shame so often enters the room.

Shame arrives with the voice of hindsight. It is the part of you that looks back once the weather has shifted and says you should have been different. You should have paused. You should have stayed calm. You should have handled that better. The word should lands like a verdict, even though it is being delivered after the fact, from a room that has already returned to clearer air.

In the moment itself, there was not yet a gap. There was not yet room for deliberation. There was a system responding the way it has learned to respond.

This does not mean you are powerless. It means your agency begins earlier than you have been taught to look for it.

Reaction

Most people try to find choice at the point of reaction, right as the words are coming out, right as the door is closing, right as the anger is rising. For many, that is already too late. The system has already committed. The room has already tightened. The weather has already pulled the nervous system into protection.

The beginning of freedom is seeing where the process actually starts.

It starts with the shift in air. The slight tightening in the chest. The narrowing of attention. The first hint of urgency that makes you want to move faster, speak sharper, fix more, control more. These early movements are easy to miss because they do not feel like choices. They feel like inevitabilities. They feel like you are simply responding to what is true.

Yet these are the moments where familiarity can grow.

With time, the place where you "arrive" to your own experience can move earlier. Not through force. Not through self-criticism. Through a gradual intimacy with your own patterns. You begin to recognise the early signs of weather before the storm gathers fully. You begin to notice the mind reaching automatically for its old evidence. You begin to sense the moment the room starts to shrink.

That recognition is not dramatic. It does not stop reactions from ever happening. It simply gives you a fraction more orientation while you are still inside it. A small awareness that something has been detected. A moment of realising the system has begun preparing. A sense that the story might be arriving faster than the facts.

Thinking Room

This is how choice eventually grows, not as a command you force on yourself in the heat of the moment, but as a capacity that develops as you become more familiar with how your system works.

When you begin to understand that reactions are often predictive rather than deliberate, something softens. You stop treating speed as a personal failing. You stop demanding perfect behaviour from a system designed to act quickly when conditions feel uncertain. You stop blaming yourself for the storm, and instead begin to recognise the weather patterns that bring it in.

The room becomes more forgiving when you stop using shame as the narrator.

The weather will still move through. The body will still respond. The mind will still reach for meaning. Yet a quieter change begins here: you start to become someone who can feel the first stirrings of a moment, rather than only meeting yourself after the fact.

Choice will come later.

For now, the task is simpler and far more humane. It is to see the mechanism as it is, and to recognise that your reactivity has a logic. You have not been failing to cope. You have been arriving late to a process that begins earlier than conscious thought.

Understanding that does not fix the moment.

It makes the moment intelligible.

And when experience becomes intelligible, it becomes easier to meet yourself with steadiness instead of blame.

Reaction

When you see this, you stop judging the reaction as if it appeared out of nowhere. You begin to sense it as part of a much larger system running the day, most of it outside conscious awareness.

That system is not only your thoughts. It's the machinery beneath them. The autopilot that keeps life moving, and sometimes keeps you braced even when the outer world looks calm.

Reflection

Think of a recent moment where you reacted faster than you wanted to. What happened?

_____

_____

What were the earliest signs — even subtle ones — that the shift had started before you reacted?

_____

_____

What tends to be your default protective move in moments like that (explain, withdraw, fix, get sharp, go quiet, people-please)?

_____

_____

If you had noticed and taken a 10-second pause in that moment, what might you have done differently?

_____

_____

When reactions make sense in hindsight, it's tempting to believe they arrived out of nowhere.

But if you slow the sequence down, something else becomes visible.

Reaction

The moment was already changing before the reaction took over.

Learning to recognise *when* that shift begins matters more than understanding *why* it happened.

Chapter Four

The System

As you start to notice the room more clearly, something else comes into view.

Most of your day is being carried by a system you will never fully see.

The thoughts you hear, the worries that loop, the moments you replay: these are not the whole of what is shaping your day. They are surface expressions of something far larger, already in motion long before you arrive at awareness.

Beneath what you consciously experience, an intricate system is carrying you from moment to moment.

Your body is not simply breathing and keeping your heart beating in the background. It is regulating temperature, blood pressure, and blood sugar. Adjusting immune responses and hormone levels. Balancing sleep pressure, hunger, alertness, and repair. Tracking posture, movement, balance, and pain.

The System

Signals pass continuously between organs, tissues, and brain regions. Chemical messengers rise and fall. Neural pathways activate and inhibit. Countless micro-adjustments are made every second to keep you upright, oriented, and alive.

None of this asks for your permission. None of it waits for your conscious mind to weigh in.

While you are deciding what to say in a conversation, your system is already answering a different set of questions.

Is this familiar or uncertain?

Does this resemble something that once required protection?

Is there enough energy available for what might be needed next?

Should resources be conserved, mobilised, or held in reserve?

These questions are not framed in language. They are answered through sensation, readiness, and tone. Through tightening or softening. Through approach or withdrawal. Through subtle shifts in how the room feels to inhabit.

What you respond to in any given moment is shaped not only by what is happening now, but by everything your system has learned about survival, belonging, and threat over time.

That learning did not begin with you.

Patterns of behaviour that once kept others safe were absorbed long before you had words for them. Ways of staying alert. Ways of pleasing, bracing, performing, withdrawing, or enduring. Beliefs formed around these patterns slowly hardened into assumptions about how the world works, and what is required to live within it.

Autopilot is not personal in the way we often assume.

It is layered.

It is inherited.

It is cultural.

It is shaped by history, environment, and repeated experience.

The system you live inside is responding not only to today's demands, but to echoes of what mattered long before today arrived.

And yet, the part of you that feels all of this rarely sees it. What reaches consciousness is much simpler.

A sense of being on edge without knowing why. A heaviness that doesn't lift, even on a quiet day. A pull to withdraw, or an urgency to push through. A feeling that small tasks require more effort than they should. These are not the problem.

They are the surface ripples of an immense amount of coordination happening underneath.

When you see this, something begins to shift.

The expectation that you should be able to think your way into ease starts to loosen. The belief that calm is a switch you have failed to flip begins to soften. The urge to judge yourself for not coping as well as you "should" loses some of its force.

It becomes clearer why telling yourself to calm down rarely works.

It becomes clearer why positive thinking can feel thin when the body is already preparing for something.

It becomes clearer why analysis, when it turns into constant monitoring, can add to the weight rather than relieve it.

Trying to understand everything that is happening inside you is not the way through. The system is far too complex for that. Chasing full understanding only pulls you back into effort.

What matters is something quieter: a willingness to *notice* that far more is happening than you ever realised.

When you allow for this, self-judgement begins to lose its footing. The demand to "do better" eases, even slightly. You stop treating your experience as evidence of personal failure and start seeing it as the output of a system doing what it has learned to do.

And something else happens too.

The moment you *notice* that much of your day is running on autopilot, you are no longer fully inside it.

Not enough to override the system, but enough to change your relationship to it. You are no longer assuming that what you feel is the whole truth of the moment. You begin to sense that the room, the weather, the stories, and the body are all moving together, responding as one.

This does not hand responsibility away. It places it where it belongs.

Not on controlling every thought or sensation, but on noticing what is shaping the system from underneath.

From here, a different question begins to form.

If so much is happening automatically, quietly, and over time, what is the system responding to most strongly right now?

That question leads somewhere very simple, and very easy to overlook. Not to thoughts. Not to emotions.

To load.

Once you sense the scale of what is running beneath awareness, another question starts to form, simple, almost disarming.

How much is my system carrying? And what happens when the account runs low?

* * *

Reflection

What shifts in you when you recognise that so much of your day is being coordinated beneath thought?

_____

_____

Where do you catch yourself treating your system like it should be a simple switch (like telling yourself to "calm down")?

_____

_____

If autopilot is layered: personal, intergenerational, cultural, what pattern do you suspect you've been living inside without realising?

_____

_____

Seeing how much of life runs beneath conscious thought can feel unsettling at first.

It raises a quieter question: if so much is already in motion before we decide anything, what is the system actually responding to?

The answer isn't willpower.

It's capacity — what the body has available, and what it's already spending, often without comment.

Chapter Five
Capacity

There are days when the room feels workable.

You move through it with a kind of ordinary steadiness. The furniture is where you expect it to be. The air is clear enough. You might be busy, even stretched, but you can still move. You answer messages without it costing you too much. You make decisions without having to rehearse them. You carry conversations. You pivot when something changes. Thoughts arrive and pass on, like background noise rather than a full performance you have to attend to.

The room is not perfect. It is simply liveable.

Then there are other days.

Nothing obvious has shifted in the outer world. The same calendar, the same responsibilities, the same house, the same people, the same routines. Yet when you step into the inner room, it feels different. The light seems dimmer. The air feels thick, as though it has been sitting still all night. The same chair holds more weight. The same tasks sit further away, out of reach, as if they belong to someone else's day.

You feel it first in small things.

Your body takes longer to rise from the couch. A simple email feels oddly impossible. Your attention slips off what you're trying to do, like your mind can't find traction. Even deciding what to eat can feel like too much choice. A shower feels like effort. A phone call feels like climbing.

On days like this, you might find yourself sitting still for long stretches without meaning to. Gazing at a wall. Scrolling without interest. Lying down without really resting. The inner room hasn't only darkened; it has tightened. There is less space to move around in, less space to think, less space to hold the normal edges of life.

This is often where the stories begin.

They arrive quietly, as if they're simply being honest.

Lazy.

Unmotivated.

Unfocused.

Flat.

Too sensitive.

Not coping.

They seem to explain the heaviness. They feel convincing, especially when the room already feels dim. The mind, in its devotion to meaning, does what it always does: it turns state into identity. It takes a day of low capacity and makes it a verdict. It takes a nervous system asking for relief and translates it into a personality flaw.

The trouble is that these stories tend to arrive at the exact moment you have the least capacity to challenge them.

When the room is already heavy, the mind reaches for the simplest explanation. It looks for something to blame. It often chooses you.

Underneath those stories, something simpler is happening.

The system has less to work with.

There is a quiet account being kept, all the time, by the body. Not in words. Not in judgement. Not as a moral assessment of how well you're doing. More like a constant internal ledger of what can be afforded: how much energy is accessible, how much effort is available, how much can be taken on before something has to give.

This is not willpower.

It is capacity.

When capacity is steady, the room feels open. You can tolerate noise, interruption, and complexity. You can hold two things at once: the discomfort and the conversation, the disappointment and the task, the uncertainty and the day. You have room inside you for a wider range of weather.

When capacity is low, the same life becomes harder to carry. The room darkens. The air thickens. Small things land as if they are larger. Sounds irritate. Decisions overwhelm. People feel like too much. The mind gets narrower, because narrowness costs less. The system becomes economical with attention, economical with movement, economical with emotional availability.

You are not becoming a worse version of yourself.

You are functioning with fewer resources.

Mood shifts alongside this, almost inevitably. When capacity drops, the inner weather often turns colder or heavier. Irritability arrives more easily. Hopelessness slips in quietly, the way dusk arrives earlier in winter. The mind begins scanning for reasons, explanations, conclusions. It flicks through old shelves looking for proof that this is who you are, that this is how life goes, that nothing will change.

The room hasn't changed in its structure.

The conditions inside it have.

This is what the body is always accounting for.

Every demand makes a small withdrawal. Some withdrawals are obvious: a poor night's sleep, a big day, a hard conversation, illness, caring for others, deadlines, noise, constant interruption. Other withdrawals are quieter and harder to name: the ongoing effort of being "fine", the background vigilance of waiting for something to go wrong, the internal bracing that you've carried for so long it feels like posture.

Then there are the withdrawals that don't look like effort at all, but cost just as much.

Holding back words you want to say.

Second-guessing every interaction.

Thinking Room

Running conversations again and again to check whether you missed something.

Keeping a social mask in place when you feel tender underneath it.

Doing the emotional maths of other people's moods.

A system can spend all day without moving very far.

Some days, there are enough resources to cover the cost. Other days, the account is already low before anything new is asked. You wake with the room already dim, the weather already heavy. You can't always tell why. You only know you are starting the day with less.

This is why stress so often forms somewhere other than where you think it does.

It is rarely the last email, the final conversation, or the small request that tips you over. Those are simply the final pebbles on a pile that has been building for weeks. The strain accumulates quietly. The system compensates without complaint. The room dims bit by bit, so slowly you adjust to it as if it's normal light.

Then one day, something small arrives.

A question.

A text.

A missed turn.

A spilled cup.

A look you can't interpret.

And suddenly it's too much.

From the outside, it looks disproportionate. From the inside, it feels like the last thread holding the room together has snapped.

When there is nothing left to draw from, everything feels like too much.

The body does not announce this with drama. It doesn't stand at the doorway and declare, You are depleted. It simply makes movement harder. Attention narrows. Energy pulls inward. The room grows still.

You might find yourself withdrawing, not as a choice, but as conservation. You might shut down mid-conversation. You might go quiet. You might stare at your phone and feel unable to respond. You might cancel plans you usually enjoy. You might feel yourself moving through the day as if through thick water.

From the outside, it can look like avoidance.

From the inside, it feels like there is no more capacity to carry what is being asked.

The mind often interprets this as failure and piles another weight on top.

Why can't I just do it?

What's wrong with me?

Why am I like this?

Those questions sound like honesty. They are usually a form of self-abandonment: a way of turning away from the truth of what your system is signalling.

Thinking Room

A different kind of understanding changes the tone inside the room.

It doesn't magically brighten the day. It doesn't make capacity appear on command. It does something quieter. It stops the room from accusing you when you are already down to the last reserves.

Low capacity can feel like a character flaw, until you see what it actually is.

A state.

A state shaped by what has been spent and what has not yet been restored. A state shaped by time, by pressure, by life lived under weather. A state that can shift again, not through forcing yourself to become a better person, but through recognising what has been true for your system all along.

When you *notice* this, the stories soften.

Not because you've argued them out of existence.

Because you no longer need them to explain what is happening.

Instead of treating the heaviness as proof that something is wrong with you, you begin to read it as information. The room is telling you something simple. The account is low. The system is doing what it must do to protect itself from collapse.

This doesn't mean you stop living.

It means you stop punishing yourself for being human.

Capacity

The body has been keeping this quiet account all along. Learning to recognise it does not add more thinking. It brings tenderness to what you are already living. It gives the room a little more truth, and a little less judgement.

The day may still feel heavy.

The room may still feel dim.

Yet something settles when you stop demanding performance from a system that is asking for relief.

And as this becomes clearer, another realisation starts to take shape.

Stress does not begin where you think it does.

It begins earlier: in the slow accumulation of cost, in the shifting of inner weather, in the quiet depletion that goes unnoticed until the smallest thing becomes unbearable.

Sometimes, when the account has been low for long enough, the inner room starts to feel haunted by its own shelves.

Thinking Room

Reflection

Think of a recent day when even small things felt like too much. What did that feel like?

What stories did you tell yourself about who you were in that state?

What do you think your system was actually asking for that day (rest, support, less input, clearer boundaries, food, sleep, connection)?

How might your day unfold differently if you could read these signals earlier, while there was still room to adjust?

Once capacity comes into view, another truth follows naturally. Depletion rarely announces itself all at once.

It builds through small withdrawals, repeated demands, and the ongoing effort of holding things together.

By the time the weight becomes obvious, it has often been gathering for a long while.

Chapter Six

Pressure

Some days, the inner room carries a heaviness that cannot be explained.

Nothing obvious has gone wrong. The calendar is ordinary. The outer world moves along as it always has. But when you turn inward, even briefly, you can feel it. The air inside feels close. Claustrophobic. As if the walls have edged inward overnight without asking permission. The light doesn't quite reach the corners. Breathing takes a little more effort than it should.

You tell yourself it's fine.

You tell yourself it will pass.

You tell yourself this is just how days are sometimes.

But the weight stays.

So you begin to move around inside your inner room.

Not to rest, but to search.

Thinking Room

You wipe dust from the nearest surface and look again. You open drawers you've opened before. You pull familiar objects into the light, hoping one of them will finally explain why the room feels the way it does. The air seems to thin with each story you touch, but you keep going. It makes sense, you tell yourself. Understanding will bring relief.

You move like an archaeologist of your own life, careful and relentless.

You dig into old layers. Childhood memories. Family stories. The things that were said out loud, and the things that were never spoken but somehow shaped everything. You remember when they laughed, and when they laughed at you. You remember trying to understand the rules without ever being given the map.

Faces begin to appear.

Crushes who never noticed you.

Bullies who noticed you far too much.

Teachers, parents, siblings, expressions frozen at moments that still don't quite make sense.

They return now as shadows along the walls of the inner room. Dark shapes in the corners you try not to look at directly. The air grows heavier as they gather.

You turn over more stones.

The things you did.

The things you didn't do.

The moments you should have known better, or believed

you should have known better, even though you were only surviving with what you had.

You revisit the roles you learned to play.

The good one.

The quiet one.

The clever one.

The agreeable one.

The invisible one.

You replay the roles of the tormentors too, not because you want to, but because they seem to hold clues. If you could just understand why they acted that way, why you were treated that way, maybe something inside the room would finally loosen.

You keep digging.

You search beneath the polished explanations and self-aware narratives. Beneath the growth you've already done. Beneath the insights you've earned honestly and painfully. You dig for the thing underneath the thing, convinced it must be there.

And sometimes, when you turn over those stones, you find things you would rather not have uncovered.

Grubs living beneath exiled thoughts.

Old shame that never learned language.

Fear that learned to hide long before you learned to name it.

The room darkens further.

Thinking Room

Not because anything new has arrived, but because the searching itself is costing more than you realise. Each story adds weight. Each interpretation thickens the air. Each attempt to explain presses the walls a little closer together.

The inner room becomes crowded with meaning.

Your body begins to respond.

Your shoulders draw in.

Your jaw tightens.

Your breath shortens, without asking permission.

The weight does not stay contained.

It rarely does.

The inner room begins to bleed into the room you are actually in. The one with other people in it. The one with faces, pauses, and consequences. Your tone shifts. Your shoulders tighten. Your responses come out a fraction sharper, or flatter, or later than you meant.

You can feel it, and so can they.

Someone gives you a little more space than usual.

A glance lingers too long.

A joke lands and no one quite laughs.

You sense the adjustment happening around you, subtle but unmistakable. The way people step back when the air feels charged. The way conversation reroutes when something is off.

You are still there.

Pressure

But you are not quite reachable.

Inside, the pressure keeps building.

The searching intensifies. The stories pile up faster now, as though urgency itself has entered the room. Your chest feels tight. Your jaw clenches. Your breath catches high and shallow, as if there is no room for it to land.

And then it happens.

The ugly mess unravels.

A sentence comes out too loud, or too sharp, or too final.

Or nothing comes out at all, just silence, that lands hard, dense and unmistakable.

An explosion, or an implosion.

The room fractures.

Then silence falls.

In the aftermath, there is space.

Just enough, and then, too much.

A thought surfaces. Not polished. Not gentle. Just clear.

What am I doing?

Air.

Not insight.

Not an answer.

Just air.

What am I doing?

Thinking Room

More space.

It's definitely too much now

Then the pressure spills out of you in whatever way it needs to. A long, shaky breath you didn't realise you were holding. A sigh that feels like it comes from somewhere old. Perhaps tears. Perhaps a heaviness settling downward instead of pressing in.

Weariness.

And grief.

And longing tangled together.

And something shifts.

Not the room.

Not the past.

Not the circumstances.

Your position.

For the first time, you are no longer lost inside the noise.

You are here, aware of the inner room, aware of the weight, aware of yourself inside it.

You're noticing.

That changes everything that follows.

Because for the first time, you are no longer lost inside the search.

You are *noticing* the inner room.

Pressure

You see the piles of stories laid open at once. The memories dragged into the light. The shadows gathered in the corners. The body slumped under the effort of trying to make sense of everything. You notice how long you have been digging. How desperately you have been hoping to find a way out.

Nothing changes in the room.

The stories do not disappear.

The past does not resolve itself.

The air does not suddenly clear.

What changes is where you are.

You are no longer inside the excavation.

You are no longer turning over stones.

You are no longer demanding answers from every artefact.

This noticing does not save the day.

It does not fix the past.

It does not offer relief on demand.

What it offers is something quieter, and more devastatingly honest: a clear view of how experience has been building. How sensation came first. How meaning layered itself on top. How stories multiplied. How the search intensified. How the body carried it all until it could not.

Seeing this does not undo the weight.

It makes it understandable.

And that matters more than it sounds.

Thinking Room

When experience is seen without blame, without the insistence that it should already be resolved, a different relationship becomes possible. The inner room is no longer something you must escape, purify, or conquer.

It becomes something you can finally stand inside without abandoning yourself.

This is the doorway.

Not to answers.

Not to improvement.

But to a new position inside your own life.

From here, the inner room does not vanish.

But you are no longer alone inside it.

Reflection

Do you recognise yourself in this scene — the searching, the digging, the need to "work it out"?

_____

_____

When you go looking for answers, what are you usually hoping to feel (certainty, relief, control, safety, permission to rest)?

_____

_____

What tends to happen to your body when you've been "in your head" for too long?

_____

_____

When the weight builds like this, it's natural to believe the answer must be buried somewhere deeper — in memory, explanation, or finally getting it right.

But something else has already begun to shift.

You are no longer only inside the search. You are starting to notice how the search itself changes the room.

From here, a different kind of understanding becomes possible, not by digging further, but by watching how meaning enters and reshapes the air.

Chapter Seven

Story

The inner room hasn't magically cleared. The shelves are still lined with old volumes. The corners still hold their shadows. The air may still feel close. Your body may still feel heavy with whatever it has been carrying.

Yet you are no longer inside it in the same way.

You are here.

Not inside the search. Not inside the urgency. Not inside the familiar compulsion to make sense of everything before you're allowed to breathe again. You are simply aware of the inner room as it is: how it feels, how it fills, how it changes without asking.

That shift is small, but it is real.

It's the moment you realise you can look around.

At first, you might only notice what hurts: the fatigue, the tightness, the old ache that seems to live in the walls. But as you stay there a little longer, something else comes into view. The room is not random. It has patterns. It has habits. It has favourite corners. It has places your attention goes without you meaning to send it there.

You begin to notice the way the atmosphere changes around certain thoughts.

A memory rises and the air thickens.

A future scene flickers and your breath shortens.

A single sentence forms and the light in the room seems to dim.

You don't do anything about it yet. You're not fixing it. You're not trying to calm down. You're simply *noticing* the sequence, almost as if weather is rolling in through a window you didn't know the room had.

And this is where curiosity begins to matter.

Because when you're noticing, you start to see that the room isn't only filled by what happens to you.

It is filled by what you reach for.

The mind has its own movements. When the air turns uncertain, it doesn't sit quietly and wait. It goes looking. It pulls something down from the shelves. It opens a familiar page. It returns to a paragraph you've read so many times your fingers could find it in the dark.

Not because you're weak.

Because your system is trying to orient.

It wants to understand. It wants to predict. It wants to protect you from being caught off guard. It wants to be ready.

Thinking Room

So it reaches for the stories that have helped it make sense before.

Sometimes the story is about what happened.

Sometimes it's about what might happen.

Sometimes it's about what you should have done, or should have known, or should be by now.

The story doesn't arrive as a story when you're inside it. It arrives as truth. As conclusion. As a lens that clicks into place so fast you can hardly feel it happening.

Yet now, from this slightly different position, you can begin to notice what the story does.

You can feel the way it changes the room.

A memory you revisit doesn't just sit on a shelf. It moves into the air. It alters the temperature. It shifts the light. It changes what feels possible. The body responds, not to the outer world in front of you, but to the meaning that has just arrived inside you.

A thought about rejection and your chest tightens.

A thought about conflict and your stomach drops.

A thought about being "too much" and your shoulders draw in.

You are watching the weather subtly change.

And at some point, the simplest and most unsettling realisation begins to form.

The inner room is not only a place you endure.

It is also a place you participate in.

Not deliberately. Not consciously. In the same way you participate in breathing without thinking about it. In the same way you participate in a mood without choosing it.

Meaning arrives.

The body responds.

The response becomes more evidence.

The evidence reinforces the story.

The story deepens the weather.

The room becomes what it becomes, moment by moment, through that loop.

For many people, this is the point where shame tries to slip back in. The mind takes the realisation and turns it into an accusation.

So it's my fault.

I'm doing this to myself.

I should be able to stop.

That isn't what this is.

This is not blame.

This is relief arriving in a new shape.

Because if the room can be shaped without your permission, it can also be influenced without force.

If the weather can change because a story took over the evidence stream, it can also change when the evidence widens again.

Thinking Room

This is where noticing stops being an idea and becomes something practical.

Not as a strategy you perform.

As a shift in what the system is responding to.

When you're lost inside a story, the story becomes the whole room. The body treats it as present. The nervous system spends as if something is happening now. It braces. It narrows. It prepares. The air thickens because the only evidence being gathered is coming from inside the loop.

When you *notice*, something else enters the room.

Not a positive thought.

Not a better interpretation.

Not a fix.

Actual contact.

The weight of your body in the chair.

The sound of a bird outside.

The feel of the floor under your feet.

The ordinary, quiet fact of this moment continuing, whether or not the story agrees.

You're still aware of the story. You haven't argued it away. Yet you have widened the room. You've added more truth to the space. The system receives a fuller picture of what's here.

That is why the weather can soften.

Not because you controlled it, but because you changed what the system had to work with.

This is the part that is easy to underestimate. It sounds almost too small to matter. Yet it matters because your nervous system is always adjusting to the evidence it receives, always calibrating, always predicting, always preparing.

When the evidence is only story, the body invests fully.

When the evidence includes the present, the body begins to stand down, even slightly.

The barometer drops a fraction. The air shifts. Capacity returns by degrees that might not look impressive from the outside, but feel like everything from the inside.

The room becomes a little more livable.

Not tidy. Not pristine. Not free of old shadows.

Livable.

A room with air in it again.

And this is where agency begins to take a gentler form.

You are not being asked to control your mind.

You are simply beginning to see the mechanism.

You can feel when your attention has been pulled back to the shelves.

You can sense when you're reading the same chapter again.

You can notice when the weather is being driven by rehearsal, replay, and prediction.

Thinking Room

You can realise, in real time, that the inner room is getting darker not because the world has changed, but because the story has taken over the light.

From this position, something new becomes possible.

Not fixing the room.

Adjusting how you are standing in it.

Noticing does not remove the furniture. It changes your relationship to it.

You stop trying to escape the room by digging deeper and deeper into meaning. You begin to live in the room with awareness present, which means the room is no longer shaped only by memory, fear, and old conclusions.

Awareness becomes part of the architecture.

And once that's happened even once, you start to recognise the doorway more quickly.

You start to sense the moment you've been pulled back into the story. You start to remember that the room can widen. That the weather can shift. That you can return to contact with what's actually here, without needing to win an argument with your mind first.

The story may still be persuasive.

The weather may still be heavy.

The day may still be hard.

Yet you have a new place to stand.

And the more often you return there, the more familiar it becomes.

Story

Not as a technique.

As a way of living.

* * *

Thinking Room

Reflection

When things feel off, where does your mind go first — past, future, or self-judgement?

_____

_____

What's one story your mind returns to often (about you, others, or what's likely to happen)?

_____

_____

What is one simple, real-world detail you could use to widen the evidence in that moment (sound, sight, feet on floor, breath, temperature)?

_____

_____

Seeing this does not make you responsible for every shift in the room.

It does something more humane.

It shows you where influence lives, not in forcing different thoughts, but in widening what the system is responding to.

Once you glimpse that, the room is no longer only something that happens to you.

It becomes something you can learn to live inside with more steadiness.

Chapter Eight

Staying

At some point, usually quietly, something becomes clear.

This room is yours.

Not because you designed it from scratch, or chose what was placed inside it, or agreed to every memory, mood, or pattern that took up residence here. It is yours in a simpler, more intimate sense. This is the inner space you wake into each day. This is where you live when you are tired, hopeful, overwhelmed, distracted, or unsure. This is where your experience gathers, whether you invite it or not.

For many people, this realisation brings a subtle unease.

If this is my room, then I am closer to it than I thought.

I can't stand outside it forever, analysing the mess or waiting for it to improve.

I'm already here.

Thinking Room

That recognition is important. It changes the stance you take.

Up until now, you may have related to your inner world as something to manage, solve, escape, or transcend. You may have spent years trying to get out of the room through insight, effort, discipline, distraction, or growth. You may have learned to stand at a distance, critiquing what you find unacceptable, or disappearing when things feel too heavy.

Noticing brings you back inside.

Not dramatically. Not all at once. Just enough to see what is actually here today.

When you look around with this quieter kind of attention, you begin to notice details you may have been stepping over for years. The room has a mood. It has a tone. It has places that feel tense, and places that feel strangely empty. There may be an old story spread open on the table, pages worn thin from use. There may be fatigue draped across the furniture, making even simple movement feel effortful. There may be a tightness hovering near the chest, or a restlessness that keeps shifting position without settling anywhere.

You are not here to fix any of this.

That impulse may still be present. It often is. The urge to tidy, explain, reframe, or motivate yourself out of discomfort can arise almost automatically.

But something else is possible now.

You can stay.

You can let the room be as it is, without turning away, and without turning against it.

Staying

This is where contact begins.

Contact is not an action you perform. It is a way of being present. A willingness to remain with your own experience without abandoning yourself, and without demanding that what is here be different before you're allowed to stay.

For many of us, this is unfamiliar territory.

We learned early on that some parts of our inner life were acceptable and others were not. Some feelings were met with care and attention. Others were met with dismissal, correction, or silence. Over time, we internalised those responses. We began to police ourselves from the inside.

When something uncomfortable arose, we demanded it change.

We criticised it for being there.

We tried to bully it into going away.

Or we left the room altogether, numbing out, staying busy, hoping distance would make things easier.

Contact moves in the opposite direction.

Contact says: *I see you.*

Not: I agree with you.

Not: you should be here.

Not: this will last forever.

Simply: *you are here, and I am staying.*

There is a particular quality to this staying. It is not passive. It is not indulgent. It does not mean giving up, or resigning yourself to suffering. It is steady, attentive, and grounded.

Thinking Room

You are present enough to know what is happening, without rushing to change it.

When you do this, something subtle begins to shift in the room.

The parts of you that have been shouting for attention often soften when they realise they are being seen. The tension held in the body for protection can ease slightly when it senses that you are not about to abandon it or attack it. The inner weather does not suddenly clear, but it becomes less hostile.

Curiosity often arrives alongside this care.

Not the sharp curiosity that interrogates or diagnoses. Not the kind that asks, What's wrong with me? or How do I get rid of this?

A softer, more human curiosity.

What is this part carrying?

How long has it been here?

What happens if I stop arguing with it for a moment?

This kind of curiosity does not demand answers. It listens. It allows things to reveal themselves at their own pace.

And that matters, because much of what lives in the inner room has learned to hide. It learned that visibility led to correction, judgement, or overwhelm. When you bring a calm, non-abandoning presence into the room, you change the conditions under which these parts exist.

The system notices.

Staying

When you are no longer bracing against your own experience, the body spends less energy defending itself. When you are no longer trying to escape the room, the nervous system does not have to keep sounding the alarm. The inner barometer drops slightly. Capacity returns in small, unremarkable ways.

This is recalibration.

Not through force.

Not through insight alone.

But through how you are with what is here.

Contact allows the room to breathe.

From this place, care begins to emerge naturally. Not as a task or a technique, and not as something you add on top of your experience. Care becomes responsiveness. Because when you are in contact, you can feel what is needed without rushing to supply an answer.

You may notice the need for rest.

Or for movement.

Or for quiet.

Or for connection.

You may notice nothing at all, and that, too, is information.

Care does not mean fixing the room. It means staying close enough to notice what the room is asking for, without insisting that it make sense right away.

This is not about staying stuck. It is about staying present.

There is a difference.

Thinking Room

When you are stuck, you are trapped inside the room, pushed around by its contents, reacting without orientation. When you are present, you are in relationship with the room. You can feel its weight without being crushed by it. You can notice its shifts without being pulled entirely into them.

Over time, this changes how the room is lived in.

The patterns that once dominated begin to loosen, not because you fought them, but because they no longer have to carry everything on their own. The stories that once ran the weather still appear, but they are not the only influence shaping the atmosphere. Awareness has joined the conversation.

This is what allows the inner world to become more livable.

Not quieter.

Not perfect.

More spacious.

You begin to recover more quickly after difficult moments. You spend less time lost in self-attack. You recognise earlier when you are overwhelmed, and you respond with less violence toward yourself. You may still struggle, still feel pain, still have days where the room feels dim and heavy.

The difference is that you are no longer alone inside it.

You are no longer trying to escape your inner world. You are learning how to remain in relationship with it.

That relationship, steady, curious, and non-abandoning, is what allows change to happen over time. Not as a dramatic

Staying

breakthrough, but as a gradual reorganisation of how you live inside your own experience.

The room does not vanish.

The weather still moves.

Life still asks what it asks.

But you are here.

And that changes everything that follows.

* * *

Thinking Room

Reflection

As you pause here, what is it like to simply be with your thoughts for a moment — without fixing or arguing?

What do you usually do when discomfort appears: push away, analyse, distract, or shut down?

What changes, even slightly, when you imagine staying, not to fix anything, but simply to remain present with what is here?

Staying offers a new perspective.

You begin to recognise the difference between being inside the room and being *with* it.

Between reacting from inside the weather and standing somewhere that allows the weather to move.

Over time, this difference becomes easier to find, even when the day tightens.

Chapter Nine
Threshold

By now, you have probably felt it.

Not as a big breakthrough, and not as a neat conclusion, but as a small shift in where you stand inside yourself.

A moment where you caught the inner room before it swallowed you. A moment where the weather moved through and you noticed it moving. A moment where the shelves started calling you back into old stories and you realised, halfway down the corridor, that you were walking there again.

These moments can be quiet. Ordinary, even. They don't arrive with certainty. They arrive with something softer.

Orientation.

You start to recognise the inner room as a place you live in, rather than a place you keep trying to escape. You begin to sense how the atmosphere changes before the story has fully formed. You can feel the way your body leans into certain meanings, the way your mind reaches instinctively for particular books, the way capacity alters what you can carry, and how quickly the room can thicken when you are already tired.

That small shift is doing more work than you realise.

It can be deeply relieving to realise your experience has shape. Patterns. Sequence. A logic to why the day feels harder some days, even when nothing on the outside looks different. It can feel like a kind of homecoming, even if it doesn't register that way at first.

And still, a glimpse is not yet a path.

This is often where people stall, without even meaning to.

They understand themselves more clearly. They can name what happens. They can see the architecture of their inner world and describe it with accuracy. They can recognise the story, recognise the weather, recognise the way the system shifts into protection.

Then life tightens again.

A conversation lands badly. A message is misunderstood. A child needs something. A work deadline presses. A tone changes. A silence stretches. A small moment hooks into something old, and the room goes dim before you have time to catch it.

Later, you look back and think, I knew this. I understood this. Why did I end up there again?

This is the moment where many people decide they've failed. That insight didn't work. That something in them is too wired, too fragile, too much.

Threshold

But what is happening is simpler than that.

Understanding helps you see the room. It doesn't automatically give you a place to stand inside it when the weather turns.

That place is built through a different kind of commitment. Not dramatic. Not ambitious. Quieter.

Crossing the threshold.

The threshold is rarely a single moment. It's a series of small returns. It's the shift from waiting for noticing to arrive by accident, to treating it as something you can come back to on purpose.

In the beginning, noticing often arrives after the fact. After you've gone too far down the shelves. After the story has gathered momentum. After the words have been said. After the withdrawal. After the inner collapse.

You find yourself in the aftermath, breathing, wondering how you got there again. And then awareness arrives.

I've been lost inside it.

Even that is a return. Even that is the threshold.

Because noticing is not a mood. It isn't a calm state you either have or don't have. It's a position. A way of standing in relation to what is happening inside you. A way of being present without needing the room to be tidy first.

Crossing the threshold means entering the room as it is.

Letting the weather be weather, without making it the enemy, and without handing it the steering wheel. Allowing the story to be there, while staying close to what else is true.

Thinking Room

The chair beneath you. The air around you. The body that is still here. The fact that you are not only the scene on the page.

At first, it can feel almost too simple to trust.

So you come back to a small question. Not to solve anything, but to orient.

What is here now?

What is my body doing?

What is the room like in this moment?

These aren't instructions. They are doorways. They don't demand that you feel better. They don't ask you to fix the past or master the future. They bring you into contact with the present moment as it actually is, which is often the first time the system receives a new kind of evidence.

This is where practice begins.

Not practice as discipline, striving, or self-improvement.

Practice as relationship.

A committed relationship with yourself.

You return, again and again, not because you have failed, but because this is how a path is formed. You return after the storm. You return in the middle of the weather. You return when you remember. You return when you forget. You return when you are tired, when you are sharp, when you are tender.

You return when it feels steady, and when it barely feels possible.

Threshold

Over time, the return begins to happen earlier.

You notice the weather change before it hardens into certainty. You feel the room tightening before you vanish into it. You catch the first reach toward the shelves, the familiar pull to excavate the past or rehearse the future, and something in you stays close enough to whisper:

I'm here.

Noticing becomes an asset.

Not because it stops the day from being what it is, but because it gives you a steadier place to stand inside it. You respond sooner. You recover more quickly. You spend less energy fighting the weather or arguing with the room. Slowly, you learn what helps you stay oriented when the air thickens.

This is the heart of *The Noticing Way*.

It isn't a method you apply to your life like a fix.

It's the way you learn to stay in relationship with experience as it unfolds.

The room will still have days where it feels dim. The weather will still move through. The stories will still appear, persuasive and familiar.

But you won't be alone inside it in the same way.

You'll know where the threshold is. You'll know how to cross it. And once you begin living from that position, the path forward tends to open in its own time, in the small, honest ways a life actually changes.

* * *

Thinking Room

Reflection

Where in your everyday life do you most want this way of being to show up? (relationships, work, parenting, sleep, decision-making, self-talk)

If you were living from a more balanced place more often, what would be the first quiet sign? (Not a big change — something small, ordinary, and noticeable.)

What might become possible if you set aside time to learn how to return to that place more reliably?

These returns don't create a new life. They change how you move through the one you have, how you speak, how you recover, how you come back to yourself when the room tightens.

The shift isn't dramatic. It's practical. You catch yourself sooner, repair more quickly, and meet the moment with a little more room inside you.

Chapter Ten

Here

Once you cross the threshold, life does not suddenly become quieter.

The room still fills. The weather still changes. The day still asks what it asks. Conversations tighten unexpectedly. Old patterns stir. There are stretches of time where the air feels heavier than you expected. Nothing about being human is exempt from this.

What changes is not the content of experience, but how you live inside it.

You begin to sense the difference between being *in* an experience and being *with* it. Between being carried by the weather and recognising it is moving through. Between being swallowed by the room and standing inside it with some orientation, even when the light is low.

This shows up first in ordinary moments.

In the kitchen, when irritation rises as the kettle takes too long.

Thinking Room

In conversation, when a familiar tightness gathers in your chest just before you speak.

In traffic, when urgency presses in and the room begins to shrink around you.

Nothing dramatic happens. There is no inner announcement. No sense that you are "doing the work". You simply recognise, quietly, that something is here.

The room may feel crowded. The air may feel heavy. A story may already be forming. And instead of stepping deeper into it, or turning away from it, you stay.

You notice the weight in your chest.

You feel the pull to explain or defend.

You sense the narrowing before the words sharpen.

Not to change any of it.

Just to remain present.

This presence has a particular quality. It is not passive, and it is not resignation. It is attentive without urgency. Curious without interrogation. Kind without trying to make anything better.

You are no longer treating parts of your inner world as intruders. The anxious thought. The tight breath. The old memory that keeps resurfacing. You meet them as what is here, rather than what must be fixed or silenced.

This is where care enters. Not as effort, but as stance.

Care shows up as not abandoning yourself when things are uncomfortable. As not bullying the room into order. As not

Here

turning the day into a personal failure because it isn't what you hoped it would be.

You stay.

You let the weather move, without pretending it isn't raining, and without demanding the sun come out. You let the room be untidy, without declaring it proof that you are doing life wrong.

Over time, this changes how the room holds you.

The edges soften, not because the contents disappear, but because nothing inside you is being shouted at or pushed away. The system spends less energy bracing against itself. Capacity returns in small, unremarkable ways.

You speak with a little less sharpness.

You withdraw with less force.

You recover more quickly after moments that once derailed you.

Not because you are doing something impressive.

Because you are no longer fighting what is already here.

Living from this place rarely looks dramatic from the outside. It looks like small returns. Gentle resets. Quiet honesty with yourself in the middle of the day.

You still feel disappointment. You still feel frustration. You still have days where the room feels dim and the weather stubborn.

But you are not lost.

You know where you are standing.

At first, noticing may still feel like something that happens *to* you.

A moment of clarity.

A pause after the spiral.

A brief sense of space when the noise settles.

These moments matter. They show you what is possible. They give you a felt sense of another way of being. But they can also feel fragile. When pressure returns, it can seem as though you have lost something again.

This is where many people quietly wonder whether noticing is enough.

The answer is not simple.

Noticing is not a solution. It is a capacity. Like any capacity, it can stay occasional, or it can be strengthened. Throughout this book, you have been discovering that another position exists. A way of standing in relation to your experience that brings orientation, steadiness, and relief. That discovery builds trust.

The next step is not to try harder to notice.

It is to recognise that this way of being can become familiar.

When noticing becomes a path, it no longer relies on chance. You stop waiting for awareness to arrive after things fall apart. You begin to return sooner. You stay a little longer. You meet yourself more consistently, especially when life tightens.

This does not mean watching yourself constantly. It does not mean analysing every thought or sensation. It means

Here

learning how to come back to the same simple contact point, again and again, when the room begins to shift.

Over time, the system recalibrates.

Attention rests more easily in what is actually here, rather than what is imagined. Sensation carries more weight than story. The inner barometer drops more readily. The body spends less energy preparing for threats that are not present.

This is not a mental trick.

It is a retraining of how evidence is gathered inside the system.

The room begins to organise itself differently, not because you are controlling it, but because presence has become part of the equation. The weather still moves, but it no longer has the whole stage to itself.

This is why noticing is best learned experientially, over time, with repetition and care. It is not about knowing what to do. It is about becoming familiar with how it feels to return.

This book has been an entry point. A way of helping you recognise the room, the weather, the stories, and the position that allows you to stay with them.

For some people, that will be enough to begin living differently.

For others, it will awaken a desire to go further. To practise this way of being more deliberately. To stabilise it under pressure. To bring it into relationships, work, and moments that matter.

Thinking Room

That desire is not a sign that something is missing.

It is a sign that something has begun.

Noticing isn't the end of the path.

It's the doorway.

And once you know where it is, you can return again and again, until staying becomes natural.

Care becomes less something you try to offer yourself, and more the way you live inside your own life

Also by Joanna Joustra

Noticing

If the *Thinking Room* helped you recognise your inner world, *Noticing* invites you to stand inside it.

This book explores how experience forms from the inside, and why overthinking is never just mental, but something felt through the body, the nervous system, and our relationships.

Drawing on contemporary neuroscience and written in reflective prose, *Noticing* follows experience as it gathers, tightens, and shifts, from early sensation through emotion, story, and action.

Guided by a river metaphor, it widens into shared water, where inner life meets relational presence.

A natural next step, to be read slowly and lived with.

The Antidote

A practical companion to *Noticing*.

The Antidote is a poetic map of common inner patterns such as self-criticism, bracing, pleasing, and withdrawal, and offers ways to meet them with clarity and care rather than through effort or self-attack.

Contact the Author

Joanna Joustra is a writer and counsellor whose work focuses on how experience forms in the body, the mind, and between people.

Grounded in contemporary neuroscience and phenomenology, her work translates complex ideas about the nervous system into lived understanding. She is particularly interested in overthinking, emotional reactivity, and the ways meaning tightens under load, often before conscious choice is available.

Joanna is the creator of *The Noticing Way*, a framework and course that supports embodied awareness, nervous system literacy, and relational presence. Her writing is reflective and experiential, inviting readers to meet experience from the inside rather than analyse it from a distance.

For counselling, speaking enquiries, or to learn more about *The Noticing Way* course:

visit: yarravalleycounselling.com.au

email: joanna@yarravalleycounselling.com.au

www.ingramcontent.com/pod-product-compliance
Lightning Source LLC
Chambersburg PA
CBHW031301290426
44109CB00012B/667